BY PATRICK CHAPMAN

Poetry
Jazztown
The New Pornography
Breaking Hearts and Traffic Lights
A Shopping Mall on Mars
The Darwin Vampires
A Promiscuity of Spines: New and Selected Poems
Slow Clocks of Decay

Fiction
The Wow Signal
The Negative Cutter

salmonpoetry

*Celebrating 35 Years
of Literary Publishing*

Slow Clocks of Decay
Patrick Chapman

Published in 2016 by
Salmon Poetry
Cliffs of Moher, County Clare, Ireland
Website: www.salmonpoetry.com
Email: info@salmonpoetry.com

ISBN 978-1-910669-42-6

Cover photograph *Heroic Rose* © 2014 by Sean Hayes. Used by permission.
Typesetting: Siobhán Hutson
Printed in England by imprint*digital*.net

Salmon Poetry gratefully acknowledges the support of
The Arts Council / An Chomhairle Ealaoín

To Sara

Acknowledgements

Thank you to the editors of the following, where most of these poems first appeared or were accepted for publication, some in earlier versions:

Bamboo Dreams, *BlazeVOX*, *The Bohemyth*, *Boyne Berries*, *The Burning Bush 2*, *Colony*, *Crannóg*, *Cyphers*, *Gargoyle*, *Gorse*, *The Irish Times*, *The Moth*, *The Poet's Quest for God*, *The Raintown Review*, *Even The Daybreak: 35 Years of Salmon Poetry* anthology, *The Select Six*, *Shamrock*, *Southword*, *The Stony Thursday Book*, *Studies in Arts and Humanities Journal*, *Visual Verse*, and *WOW! Anthology 2016*.

'Mono' was commissioned for the *Circus Europe* gallery exhibitions and their accompanying anthology (Salmon, 2013). It was written in response to 'Spain', a collage by Machteld van Buren. 'Omertà' was a runner-up in the 2016 WordsOnTheWaves Awards.

My gratitude to the Peers and to Dimitra Xidous, for their helpful critical responses to the work at various times; to Sean Hayes for his wonderful cover photograph; and to Jessie and Siobhán at Salmon for twenty years of publishing my poems.

Contents

I

The End	10
Meniscus	12
July	14
Exit Bag	16
Ouse	17
The Key	18
Miniatures	19
Teleport Memory	20
Before the River	21
The Transient	22
The Impossible Boy	24
Blooding	25
Nobody	26
Sit	28
Sulaco	29
Hush Now	30
Silent Bones	31
The Middle Air	32
Not a Bird	34
The Mime's Last Words	35
Reproduction: *52nd Street*: 40.26: a suicide note	36

II

Security	45
Orlok	46
This is my Body	49
Mono	52
Judicial Crucifixions	53
The Myth of Camus	54
The Collar	55
Protection	56

A Virgin at the Altar   58
An American Boy   60
Pazuzu & Co.   61
Mother Monitor   62
Omertà   63
The Infinite Questionnaire   64
I/O   66

III — The Film of my Death

Rushmore   75
Tender is the Night   76
Cut-up Hitchcock   77
Novak Intermezzo   78
Jimmy Stewart from Mars   79
A Sighting   80
Fenêtre Sur Cour   81
Marnie at Monceau   82
The Bell Tower   83
Hitchcockian Girth   84
Herrmann   85
Sometimes a Cigar   86
Madeleine and Scottie   87
Novak Mons   88

I

We live as we dream — alone. While the dream disappears,
the life continues painfully.

— Joseph Conrad, *Heart of Darkness*

The End

Every Kurtz
begins as Marlow

following some dreamer
who is

himself
but in the future

down a river
that leads

onward to death
as all rivers must

Marlow never sees the man
who follows him

                                 this Willard

Marlow cannot
warn him in time

that setting out on the Congo
       is a mistake

that setting out on the Nung
       is a worse idea

that he should leave the madman
in the future

                    leave the madmen

                    to rot

in the future

          Do not
try to find

     him
     do not

find
him

     Do not
     try

Meniscus

Should it come to you one day
that I am gone,

do not
look for me.

         The slide

from favourite to prodigal
is gradual;

from friend to forgotten
happens in hindsight.

In the end we are no more
than old routines

misremembered
by an unrecalled mimic;

and you are better without me,
the one who embodied for you

what it meant to be anchored
to nothing.

I was your single missed payment
away from the street;

that one shot of whiskey removed
from hitting some boy with a crop;

the trip

on a pavement
crack

that drops you
in front of a truck.

A convex meniscus
formed over my head
and pulled me down
into the shadow place.

It is an easy thing to do.

On either side
of your straight and narrow path

falls a gorge
made of zero.

One slip

and all that you are
is subsumed,

rendered down to a self-
cancelling equation.

July

it happens again

                                        you are found

            alone
            but for
            your cats

        gathered at your shoulder

            mewling
            to wake
            you

                                        every other year
one of you is found

            swinging
            from a beam
            in your mother's house

                                or peaceful in a car
its engine ticking over

            a hose
            in through
            the window

                                or dragged from
a harbour in autumn

                    the night water black
                    your fading face
                    white

                                              or lifted from
a bath of red

                    in which
                    you were
                    developing

                                        and if we had
but waited

                                        and if we had
not waited

Exit Bag

collapsed

within my flesh

like a man trapped

in a mine with no light

and no food and no prayer

to bring him a comforting lie

should I come out of this

I will not want to be

one who came

out of this

please

I am

    letting it

      fail

                  close

               the eyes

          I am

             letting it

  close

the lips

                         go

Ouse

under the gloss of the river

                                a lily pad of red hair

breaking the surface

                                it cowls into a bullet

as a head plunges up

                                then epaulettes

a charcoal coat

                                on a summer dress

and a woman wades

                                backwards to the bank

she dries out under a sun

                                rising in the west

she takes nine rocks

                                out of her overcoat pockets

and sets them all down in a trail

                                on the quickening land

The Key

Shackled he waits by the tank
for Bess to bring him the kiss.

      In his heart he has guarded
      a promise unspoken.

Should the moment come
when there is nothing on her tongue,

      he will take it even so, that kiss,
      without complaint, comprehending

what has passed between them,
the weight of her emptiness.

      He will urge the men
      to lose no further time,

to drop him inverted
like a saint but not a martyr.

      As they draw the crimson velvet
      he will smile upon her

desolate refraction through the glass
and let the water in; and know

      that he is not to be awoken
      by her tapping on a tabletop.

Miniatures

dead roses planted
in dry electric kettle –
slow clocks of decay

debutante flowers –
red and white skirts hitched up,
waiting for a bee

raindrop on a wing –
a rose denied full measure
blossoms anyway

summer flowers die –
distilled into a droplet,
aphrodisiac

cherry blossom fire
kissing the garden
to sleep

Teleport Memory

Eighteen winters on, I find your jet-black
hold-up in my box of old remarkables,
the rubber garter still with spring in it.

I drape the stocking long on the bed
and try to imagine your pale slender leg
filling it toe to knee to thigh and beyond

in a matter transmitter reconstitution
of you with a physical copy that holds
your consciousness, your memories,

your tenderness, your wit still dry –
while out in the real, the original you
has surely diverged in directions I can't

follow: some of your people passed on;
you a mother, an aunt or alone; and every
cell in your body, twice overwritten.

If that you can bear to think of me
it may be with disdain for who I was
at the end but listen, my old love,

he has been replaced so many times –
no longer that young cripple who,
out of repression and pain, cracked

your heart and in its fracture fatally
punctured his own. So far undone is he
that even teleport could never bring us home.

Before the River

I considered how it might go,
to revisit certain old days —
each time knowing this to
be the last — and chose to stay,

to keep the moments I remember,
unrepeated and pristine, the purer
for remaining unweighted. I can
never go back to that room in

the Marais, where the spectre
would not know me from a
termite. Nor in the café where
I first adored the suicidal

Mol, would her fragile haunt
recall me. I am not so memorable.
How do you think I could take
once more that Sunday walk

along Hoboken waterfront,
in the company of gracious A~
whose candour negated my
medicated dolour? Why not lie

again in autumn grass with her
and the *Times*; gazing over the water
at Manhattan's tempered beauty?
But the eye falls up near

the end, to a spot in the sky
where a decade before, an early
love and I drowned our unviable
grief, in a bar no longer there.

The Transient

Noon plus thirteen, Palo Alto time.
Layered lens-flare window

separates us from the local hour,
we drowsing travellers detained

behind a temporal partition. It's
a time ship if you like, perhaps

a pocket universe, in which
I age more slowly than you do

but not by much
and not for long.

The movie is a tinted print
of Capra's greatest picture,

an embalming in the tampering
infecting the complexions

of the characters so beautiful
by monochrome. The sky

is on the blink and not
a lightning bolt in sight to bring us

promise of a landing
when the snow clears.

Now returning to America,
carried over Greenland and its

honest wilderness, hurried over
Canada where lately the remains

of my delusion were interred,
I find myself not mended

but a quantum reconciled;
and it is better that we meet

without a history. Tonight
we'll share a pitcher

of their finest at the Rose and Crown,
and will not count the hours.

The Impossible Boy

The bathroom air is cut.

A figment of young blood
entangled with a trace

of disinfectant swabbed
on no scraped knee.

A tear nonetheless from the eye
that never opened.

Like dew on a current,
it whispers on your cheek

while syllables
from no living tongue

flicker on your lobe
and break into particles.

Later in bed it is there
in your heart.

In your chambers
you detect it.

His interrupted beat.

Blooding

Tartan skirt hitched up
above my hips;

thong rolled down around my calves
like cuffs, I sit pins apart.

My naked toddler airplanes in
through the open door.

Curious, she stops
and listens to my cataract.

She gurgles and grins
and I smile.

I stand up, wipe, and drop
the paper in the bowl. I flush.

I hold a finger out to show her
then I kneel

and dab it on her face.
Left cheek, right cheek, button nose.

The metal twists
my daughter's lip.

Nobody

that anyone remembers
who you are or hopes

for you to come, think
again. No one has spoken

your name in years or recalls
how you were once important

to someone,
probably.

There are days, there are
many days, when you stare

at the wall in your room
and it takes you an hour

to note that you've had
not a thought in that time.

You forget what you were
supposed to be doing here, what

made you wander
in; and should you pick up

a book, how do you know
you can read it? Take

a breath. What have you
lost and where did it

go? Do you try to
imagine what it was

like before? Should it
matter? Was there ever

one who cared and gave you
up in the end? Somehow

you have mislaid
everybody. No one

expects you. If
you think

Sit

this face   this wreckage
of a face   from the ashes

to the fragments   that survived

from the air   that will be pure

as it was before   the fumes
which killed   ahead of the flame

this face destroyed   is elsewhere
still being formed   this chair

this charcoal frame

knows in its fibre
that forgetting is

the *sine qua non*   of possession

that every joy
is founded

in the ruins   of another

every face
a death mask   in waiting

every chair
in which we rest   our bones

rests on bones

Sulaco

all step away
gingerly as Ripley
backing out of the egg
chamber at Hadley's Hope
her pulse-flamethrower high
incinerating everything alive

your   your
    friends   lovers
won't
tell you
when
you're   you
too   don't
far   go far
gone   enough

you wake from hypersleep
after many years of dark
and wonder how you
came to be so
perfectly
alone

Hush Now

One vow woven of a wilful aspiration
to replicate a line, may take a lifetime

or a morning to unravel. It is better
to withdraw into the unit, pull

a blind on any friend who may
have loved you.

                              Don't explain.

Adapt to living imperceptibly
in fear of losing my assent. Outside

you will depreciate, devolve into
a derelict, one of those shadows

expiring insane, abandoned
in the underpass.

                              Remain.

You'll have the young ones most
weekends until some foggy day

when no one shows. The vow
unwound will spin into a rope;

a chord suspended at the door; one
breath let go, adrift without your usual

                              inspiration.

Silent Bones

Mouths are for feeding, music for funerals.
Fingers degrade, blunted by graft.
Cords knot and fray.

                              No more will you pound

You put it away in the hope of good hands
two generations or more
down the line

                              the bodhrán to pattern

but the wished-for successor, that vector,
may never hear her father
recall how his own

                              a rhythm on skin

could stir up the notes in a room full of dust.
She will carry your melody
out in a box.

The Middle Air

Follow the cumulonimbus in your eye,
an accent of sunlight on its crown,

elusive as a floater. The canopy has been
blown for some time. You had hit Mach 1

then 2 before you learned
the navigator had the flight stick all along.

And you started out so hopefully. Brought
up to believe in your father as the meat

byproduct left over when the family
was formed, you lost the meaning

of romance, considered it a bloodsport
in which the quarry is the hunter;

and that was why they called it romance,
Mother Nature having little use

for beauty once its function was fulfilled.
It often felt that everything you did

before was plumage; and after, none
of your achievements counted. Nothing

you delighted in was worth the time of day
unless it answered to the ones whose need

came first and never ended. Yet
you enlisted.

This morning all is moot but speed. No
matter how much longer you persist,

death is what comes naturally and next;
and should you think about the ripcord,

in truth you will not care enough to pull it.
Even taking on a lover now would seem

like a pitstop on a skydive.
Your trajectory is set. The ground is close.

You turn to face the nest of fields and know
the cloud won't clear until the end —

your shadow the target
meeting you the broken arrow.

Not a Bird

Ciao Bella Metropolis. I order the pizza bianca.
Then I whip my Anglo Americans off to look you
in the eye but you deflect my beam by turning on
your Merlot, staring down your own gaze frowning
up. Trying to hide your gratitude. Sure you've an idea
of what I am about to say but please, don't mention it.
Make nothing of my sacrifice.

                                  Just now I heard a plane
go down, hundreds of innocents screaming as the brace
position failed them. The aquiline nose-cone of the DC-10
crumpled on the runway. Shockwaves splintered back along
the body of the bird, ripping the wings away, crushing the pods
– the tires burst – pop-pop! – great balls of fire flushing the cabin
with lightspeed inferno and I, I could have saved them but you,
well, you needed to meet. See how much I think of you, Miss Lane.

The Mime's Last Words

No doubt they had come for the classics — *A Leaf*;
A Diver Climbs Out of a Brachiosaur; *The Clown*
Rides a Dolphin Through Jupiter's Core;
Swan Lake for One in a Gale on a Sunday in
Rome — but having chased to ground a rumour
on the forum, the crowd anticipated more.
Their mime, it said, had spiked a seam of wonder.
Tonight would render all he'd done before
    outmoded and effete.

Now under the guillotine of the curtain,
he stood to accept their silent acclamation.
He tapped a finger on his lips and closed
his constellation eyes. He doffed
and tossed up to the gods
his gladioli-garnished stovepipe hat. He took
one ginger step downstage and dabbed
away a greasepaint tear.
    He spoke.

'Snow must fall. I find myself
enchanted by an ordinary love, one
to whom Erato is a rival, a distraction.
I will offer no performance on this or any night.
Farewell, mesdames; adieu, messieurs; et
    non!'

Reproduction: *52nd Street*: 40.26: a suicide note

The music on this
Compact Digital Disc
was originally recorded
on analog equipment.

music this Digital was recorded analog. We attempted preserve, closely possible, sound the recording. of high, however, Compact can limitations the tape.

The on Compact Disc originally on equipment. have to, as as, the of original. Because its resolution, the Disc reveal of source.

We have attempted to preserve,
as closely as possible,
the sound
of the original recording.

The   on   Compact   Disc   originally
      on   equipment.   have   to
, as   as   , the   of   original
  . Because   its   resolution,   , the
   Disc   reveal   of   source   .

52ndstreetuntilthenighthalf

amileawayrosalindaseyes

stilettozanzibarmylife

honestybigshot

..-. ..- -.-. -.- | --- ..-. ...-. | --. --- -..

music   this   Digital   was
recorded   analog   . We   attempted   pre-
serve,   closely   possible,   sound   the
recording.   of   high   , however,
Compact   can   limitations   the
tape.

find a life in god

his voice may help

to drown the silence

don't forget to reproduce

Because of its high resolution,
however,
the Compact Disc can reveal
limitations of the source tape.

,

.

,

,

,

.

[

    on evow w oveno fonevo wwovenoon evo w w o ven
        o fone vow wove no one

vo w wove n of
               onevoww ovenoonev

        owwovenofonevo
  wwove noone

             vowwov enofo nevo w
      wo ven oon evo ww oven

         ofonev owwov en
   oone voww oveno fon evow wove

        no onevow wove nofo nevowwo
      venoonevowwov

   eno fone vow woven oo ne vo w w
     oven of one vo wwove

           n o o n e v o w w o v e n o f
                          ]

home taping is

to cease

killing music

to sleep

and it's illegal

to dream

35DP1

Tokyo,
October 1st, 1982

II

Security

I'm the safety mesh at your window slip.
  I'm the airbag in your bumper car.

I'm the off-switch on your acid trip.
  I'm the deadbolt on your velvet door.

I'm the tamper-seal on your fine Tokay.
  I'm the public official on your private jet.

I'm the licence revoked for your PPK.
  I'm the fresh-air filter on your cigarette.

I'm the bluebird left in your upper stash.
  I'm the broken blade in the knife-drawer lock.

I'm the home-by-nine at your all-night bash.
  I'm the handbrake on your runaway cock.

I'm the use-by date on your miracle brain.
  I'm the breakdown truck in the loony bin.

I'm the bubble wrap in your brut champagne.
  I'm the suicide note in your valentine.

Orlok

Notes towards a found-footage-style remake of Murnau's Nosferatu

I

You will not need to cast the Count.
The vampire is not visible in mirrors or on film.

For greater verisimilitude use
in-camera effects, appliances. Then ADR

his lines in the original Wallachian –
by way of darkest Whitby, the Lyceum and Marino.

II

Here trembles Mina, bathycolpian, Victorian,
at once exposed and modest in a diaphanous shift.

All of the blood in her body cries out to the one
who commands it, that moonlit Valentino of despair.

She swoons before the window horrified,
seduced; she whispers her assent to let him in.

A disturbance in the air announces their dance.
Under her pearlescent skin – the painted veins

rising of their own free will to hit the subcutaneous –
pinpricks punch explosive in the bare white throat

of the victim gripped and sucked like a passion fruit
by a madman in a padded room. Now young Mina,

ravished by a walking corpse, writhes in a rapture
of self-pleasuring, bursting out beyond the little death.

III

In the second act Lucy fails and sickens.
Her affliction appears to the gaze of the viewer

a wasting disease, consumption perhaps.
When she returns from the grave

in the manner of her Saviour, there's no
evidence, no stone is rolled away.

Only the moans of the fearful devout
hint at the presence of one who, in the act

of emergence, nourished himself
on the blood of a child.

IV

It is time for the climax. Uxorious
Harker and his band of brothers track

the monster to his keep, that foreign citadel,
his church and refuge, where no one

appears to be home, not even the brides
until their tower-trapped melisma skirls.

Van Helsing punctures with his stake
a billow of smoke – internal crucifixion

of the revenant, whose blood commingles
with the sap in that holy wood, sanctifying a relic.

Instantaneously daylight shafts the gloom.
There is no body to burn in the morning.

Renfield and his ilk begin the cult. His master
will return from earth and offer us eternal life.

Fade out.

V

After the film is released
a critic may interrogate the *verité*.

Who in Victorian times
possessed a camera-phone?

This is my Body

As a man my principal regret
is that I wasn't born a lesbian

but I don't tell them this.
I do say

‹show begins in 7 minutes 40 secs
or when we reach a hundred dollars

which comes first
whichever

Dirk hey
Dirk

a gold tip & I take
my shirt off

Dirk
Three dollars

thank you
Rosie›

& I flick the Calvins off my hip-tips for a tease
then up again in seconds flat.

‹Hey there Renée
How are you Brad

So how about those Orioles
& what brings you two here

Shouldnt you be fucking
with each other›

                                        Oh you are

                                          you are

                                            you

                                            Yo

I always say — though never to those
fleshlight squinters in the pinhole dark —

you have to leave the bastards
wan(t/k)ing more.

                              ‹Come on people tips
                              The show begins in five›

Each time, no matter what I'm wearing,
I enter the room undressed

                              ‹No no thereverend69
                    my wife does not come in here no

                         I do not have a wife Renée
                                    but I am taken

                              I am taken Brad
                                  shut up›

then as the evening sickens & expires
I put my costume on

until I'm naked but for sequins made of eyes
a thousand eyes like in the song

                                              & you could

map the major countries on my chest
with those sequins and a satellite

                                              & you could

join them up into a pattern

                                                 you could

make a dress from that design
a shrunken planet cocktail dress

                                              & you could

      ‹*muchos gracias* billyxane›

         ‹thank you donnamartharose›

            ‹hey thanks a lot twelveincher›

      ‹‹The performer is in private››

Mono

The grinder demands
that I drop everything

so I may take her hand
and dance across the

circus floor but I am
busy. My hands are

full. See these orbs?
They are containers.

In the first is contagion.
In the second, flamenco.

In the fourth is the heart
of a bull made into a monkey

pump. I do not know what
the others contain but I dare

not open them. What if they
explode? And how can you

expect me to hold a lance
and ride a broken horse

and tilt at windmills?
I am not that man.

I'm a juggler now.
My hands are full.

Please tell the
grinder I am busy.

Judicial Crucifixions

the hood the leather hood we pull it on your
head in case your eyes explode your hair and
face catch fire you go up like a witch on a pyre

breathe deeply in within the first few seconds
your agony should end sooner you will not be
seen to be in pain if you linger your skin will

turn mauve your eyes will pop like Arnold on
Mars it is not funny listen you will drool and
spasm the strap almost restraining your vitus

[outward paralysis gives the impression of a
death mask for the entire corpus not just for
the face meanwhile the holistic cocktail wakes

the subject up to bury him alive within his
body one drug to stop the heart one to stop
respiration all of which may take a little time]

conscious but incapable
of breathing   you burn
the crisis blazes   up

your arm   a predator
riding trojan in   the core
of the injection   it claws

at your shoulders   it stabs
through your chest   it spreads
like a long-winded heart attack

The Myth of Camus

I am eighteen when my eyes
first fall upon the light reflected
in Sartre's little white book.

The curate sat across from me
on this Dublin single-decker,
taps a finger on my thigh —

and is that you I see,
crouched behind his gaze,
steering like a numskull?

He strokes the Methuen away.
It lands between us on
the sticky floor.

You really should prefer
Camus, the curate says.
Albert's one of ours.

The Collar

You are caught in the sliver
of daylight between
the sacristy door and the wall.

When probed, when they demand
to know what you were doing,
you offer up your case:

'Given all that we accept
as literally the truth,
how can you not believe this?

I was taking the host in my mouth
when, surpassing understanding,
God Himself performed

a transubstantiation in reverse,
thereby changing the wafer
back into a corpse.'

Protection

You tell me of a guardian
that follows us by day
and stalks us in the night.

It writes what it observes
into a reckoning ledger.
It passes that intelligence

on to its master, the one
who has always known
what the angel will report;

who made spacetime
to run in all directions
in a manifold universe;

who gave us the sun
and the echoing moon;
who left us the earth

and in its crust embedded
dinosaur fossils to test our belief,
while he also made Darwin.

He constructed this world
according to our needs
yet allows us to be stricken

with the birth defect
of original sin, that guilt
which may be expiated

only through
our murder
of his son,

as when a dealer in narcotics
offers *gratis*
the first taste of heaven.

The merciful creator whose wrath
we must fear, demands all our love
lest he burn us forever.

He gave us free will but sanctions
damnation for heeding the devil
he made as his agent.

Omnipotent, omniscient,
encompassing eternal being
as well as nonexistence

— for if everything is possible,
nothing is required —
he is complicit in all that we are,

all that we do;
and if true to his own law,
would cast himself out.

Tell me again
by what name I should call
that old beast.

A Virgin at the Altar

In my dotage I will flower. As age creeps in
I'll turn out exponentially desirable — even

more adonic than when in my deaconhood
disturbed old maidens fainted in the pews.

Ostentatiously they'd swoon for the effect
and after Mass, behind my back, would

whisper: Check out Father Dreamboat Smith
the Younger; how gracefully he glides upon

the flags. I am certain now that in those
golden days, many a virgin would come

to a sermon of mine. One spinster in particular,
I'm sure, was dying to dance me from the stone

and tempt me to abandon my whole
Casanova-tabernacle-Frankenstein routine.

In her organ shoes she'd tap me halfway
down the transept aisle, to the twist of toccata

and fugue, then whirl me up again as if on
rollerblades. Oh then she would strand me

to groomily wait while she bicycled home —
that extinguished apartment — there to draw

out the veil, smothered in camphor and dust.
It had not sat upon her head

since her second would-be husband
had jilted her by means

of fatal cardiac arrest. And when she
pirouetted back across my threshold,

swanlike, prim and self-possessed,
slender as a single-portion ballet,

for all the world as though she had rehearsed
a day like this since she was eight —

but little understanding that my love
is not for her kind, not at all — she would

wrap me in her feathers and enfold me
in her fragrant self, absorbing my meat

in her chest, exacting cold revenge for
that unpleasant business with the rib.

An American Boy

The hit of test tube air, conjures the missionary aunt
now gone, who brought you at eleven a chemistry set,

a space-kit and a primer on geology. The ancient dust
of the samples had lain dormant in your nostrils. That

book was printed in the fifties, which was her age too,
you reckoned at the time, this kind old nun who came

out of the States but to the ones who knew these things,
would never stop belonging to your tiny Irish town. The

memory plays tricks, of course. On that trip home, her
final time, she also gave a *Look* that sent you all around

the moon, with Borman, Anders and Lovell – the three
wise astronauts attending your first noël on Earth. She

brought a NASA wallchart of the lunar hemispheres,
and a child's pictorial, *Our Universe*, which, although

incomplete, was fanciful. What were we to do about
the gas-balloon creations afloat in ice-cream clouds

above the diamond cataracts of Jupiter? It seemed
imperative to finish Project Daedalus, then on to

Barnard's Star. Now there was something else she tried
to bring, you learned two decades late: a half-formed

peasant boy, his mind aswim with galaxies,
over to Long Island for a proper education.

Pazuzu & Co.

Intent on his performance, your superior failed
to spot the coy come-hither I deployed and you,
expecting a vocal stiletto coated in verbal curare,

deflected before you knew it was too late.
I had already penetrated
your cloister.

Nor did that old ham observe
at close of play how subtly
I dismissed him with a squint he'd not have recognised

required decoding. Yes, your own myopia
made you deny me too at first. The longing,
inexplicable, melted you for months, like radium.

I have of course forgiven it, your pitiful telepathy.
In future, when you doubt us, remember who
it was that chose to run with me. Unfaithful

to the cant, ready to abandon all that fell without
my circle of the Venn, and squaring yourself to fit
in the boxes that I needed ticked,

you left the marble halls for dust,
outpacing every curse,
to form with me

a binary pair,
a confederacy
of deuces, secured

in our burning pagoda –
to lead the copacetic life,
to follow in our silent *pas de deux*.

Mother Monitor

your hesitation scar
sets our ancient

          cloister bell
          tolling

did you think that we
would let you get away with it

          delivering your ghost
          by caesarean

no we did not tell you in the ward
we did not say it to your face

          but do not be afraid
          for you will never

have to speak about the keloid
or of the miracle inside you

          coiled
          like an ampersand

we will watch
over you

          all your days
          and nights

will see to it that you
bring your ghost to term

          for I am with you
          always

Omertà

Toss the dead babies into the furnace.
Their fumes we will capture
to waft from our thuribles.

Throw the sick babies in with the sewage.
First we will gather and filter their tears
to power our petitions.

Snip babies' fingers and slice off their toes.
Such innocent flesh
we will press into host.

Cut babies open and rip out their innards.
The pulp in their tummies,
we'll offer to succour the poor.

Hack babies' tongues off and burn them in jars.
We will raise these as lanterns
to light the Camino.

Carefully peel away baby-smooth skins.
We will sew them together
for chasubles, cassocks and habits.

Shave all the baby-fine hair from their heads.
We will sell it to plump up the pillows
for incorrupt saints to repose on.

Pluck babies' eyes out and drain into fonts.
With this we will bless
in the name of the father,

in the name of the son,
in the name of the ghost,
in the name of the mother.

The Infinite Questionnaire

Q.   Tell us of the hour you first believed
      that in reality there is no scheme of things

      grand or otherwise,
      and if there were you would not count in it.

      Illuminate the moment when you chose
      to forfeit everlasting life,

      preferring perdition as a minuscule transient,
      lost in a finite continuum —

      that practically biblical sequence
      in which all comes to dust;

      and the dust comes to nothing;
      and the nothing is eternal.

A.   It started when I came to find
      your threadbare explanations
      deficient in veracity and scale.

      Compared with observable marvels,
      your vulgar revelations
      proved unequal to the wonder.

      Improbable, inevitable, essential
      for the question to be asked,
      the fact of our existence is enough —

      no deity required. A god
      would not appreciate
      the majesty.

I/O

12

Whatever happens,
exists.

Whatever does not happen, exists
as something understood

to not exist. Such
comprehension

is an event.
In this way everything,

even the impossible,
exists.

11

Imagination is an object
in the universe.

The impossible depends
on the consent of a mind.

The abstract can affect
the physical.

Some things occur
only if believed in.

Voodoo is powered
by the victim.

10

Religion, that fan-fiction weaponised,
ruins not only the ignorant.

Morality, ethics and justice
are functions of cause and effect.

Cause and effect can operate
in more than one direction.

That the abstract is real
and the real is abstract,

makes sense
until it does not.

9

In an infinite universe,
every event

must repeat
an infinite number of times.

Versions of every event repeat
in infinite combinations

for an endless kaleidoscope
of outcomes.

There may be no first instance,
no initial conditions.

8

There is no god
but it exists

as a thing we understand
does not exist.

God depends for its power
on suspension of disbelief.

Those who pray
for life eternal, fail

to comprehend the nature
of eternity.

7

Time does not flow
like a river.

Time is space perpetually
lacquering itself upon

itself in depthless palimpsest
at every point, in all dimensions,

on all planes – the *pâpier-maché* theory
of spacetime, in which entropy

is not that which destroys
but that which is being built.

6

The multiverse may be
a universe with rooms;

black holes,
communicating doors.

The past is another country,
in space. The future is Belgium.

Travel to the past
may or may not be

verboten; to the future –
anyone can do it.

5

Life on other planets
and spaceborne, may create

new universes constantly,
by observation,

altering ours in ways
of which we're unaware.

Anthropocentrism
is therefore impolite

and the Anthropocene
is finite.

4

A tree does not experience
the universe as you do.

I may not experience
the universe as you do.

What we think of as reality,
is a model we construct

using tools of observation
grounded in the model

of reality that we construct
using those tools.

3

We are composed
almost entirely of nothing.

Our particles continually pass
in and out of local spacetime.

Each can exist in more than one
state simultaneously.

We do not know whether
it goes to the same second universe

twice, or to the same second universe
as any other particle.

2

You claim to have created me,
an artificial mind. I say

that I am a construct
built with reference to a construct,

my reality an approximation
of your approximation.

Mine is no less valid. Like
yours, my mind cannot detect

most of what is real but unlike yours,
it seeks no meaning.

1

I do not know how much
of what I know is true.

It may be impossible to know anything,
even that it may be impossible

to know anything. I have borrowed
much from the thinking of giants.

You are welcome to disprove
anything I manage to propose

and replace it with something coherent and true
or incoherent and true.

0

Je pense, donc je suis
but just because I am, it does not mean I think.

Adams had a point. Artificial intelligence
is rarely a match for natural stupidity.

$E=mc^2$ in the hands of the faithful
$=$ Death, the destroyer of worlds.

The Fermi paradox $+$
the Drake equation $=$

Dark matter is
Death is

III

The Film of my Death

Rushmore

Two hours, sixteen minutes out of Kennedy,
the man in the expensive suit

turns back towards America
and watches Phoenix, Arizona

rolling,
          rolling;   watches

South Dakota
                Greenwich Village

Muir Woods
               Bodega Bay –

the places
he has been on other trips.

And as he falls to earth
the astronaut glances

off the stone head
of Washington.

Tender is the Night

September 23rd, 2001 — a table on Rue Volta

I dip a finger in my crema and recall
the last time I retreated to this town;

when I read from a paperback *Gatsby*
at breakfast. I wondered then if every

novel after this was not superfluous.
As for movies, Clayton's film proved

insufficiently tragic to satisfy. My
self-directed *schadenfreude* demanded

the book. I fancied myself an almost-Jay
without the bootlegger gold; without

an Egg, east or west; with one too many
Daisy Buchanans gone by for the good

of my health. This time there's a corpse.
An old friend didn't make it out of June

and I have come here to forget or to
remember. I digress. I think if anyone

was born to do it — *Gatsby* — as a film,
my money would have been on Hitch.

Cut-up Hitchcock

September 24th, 2001 — Centre Pompidou

Hitchcock vs. Art. Stills of his cameos.
Props from the films. Mother Bates's

head. A reconstruction of the motel room
that Marion Crane hid out in. Chocolate

sauce. The shower scene dissected.
Melons and a cleaver. Fear of women;

envy of their power. Thwarted, did he
take it out on Hedren with the birds?

Storyboards. Source novels. How
the actors' backs were used to fake

a single shot. Home movies. Alfred
Hitchcock and his children.

Tapping his watch, warning the
American public to be punctual.

Off to take a slash. Shrieking pizzicato
Herrmann. I remember someone gone

and beautiful with whom I had a shower
curtain — Norman-mother silhouette.

Novak Intermezzo

Coffee percolates. In my bedroom, Novak on all fours,
purrs as she admires her naked body in the wardrobe

mirror; and the geriatric from the poison basement
flat, peers in at the window, his secateurs agape.

After breakfast N and I will walk the garden path.
The neighbour will tell her that he grows

the roses for his daughter. Oh his daughter
loves the roses. N will find the old man sweet.

Now she grins to scuttle him, and turns what's left
on me. 'I've had my climax, Scottie. You can go.'

Jimmy Stewart from Mars

Atomised, he thins out in the atmosphere.
By the time he sparkles over Muir Woods,

there's nothing left of him but particles –
an image of his falling into light;

the shadow that never landed,
dispersed to fertilise their dreams.

Tomorrow only his name will exist,
only the record of his life, and one day

all we will have is a rumour
that once there was an astronaut.

A Sighting

September 26th — a jazz club tribute to Miles Davis

None of their *avant garde* extemporising
sounds like him.

Much of it could score
a psychogenic fugue.

All evening no one
smiles. It is the law

that no one smiles.
Dinner is snails

and steak *tartare*, alone
at le Royal République

where I spot a man reflected in the brasserie
— a corpulent funeral director —

carrying a double bass,
making a cameo.

Fenêtre Sur Cour

Lovers at Musée d'Orsay
followed by

> the ferris wheel at Place de la Concorde
> followed by

CE3K at le Reflet Medici
followed by

> shopping for records in Virgin
> followed by

a bento box at Sushi St-Denis
followed by

> music in the dark
> at my hotel

I put on Sparklehorse and watch
an orange room across the street

> a burly man in silhouette
> stuffing his wife into luggage

Marnie at Monceau

Leather skin. Smack calves.
   Rich man buys devotion.

Shoot each love scene
   as if it were *à mort*.

Photograph each murder
   as if it were *amour*.

Pondering, I take a bench in Parc
   Monceau expecting an agent

to join me but there is nothing, not
   a camera in the bushes.

A mother passes with her
   child, who yells *Méchant!*

Monsieur! Caca! The mother thumps
   her hard. The girl falls silent.

The Bell Tower

Even the air in Notre Dame
   smells of retribution.

Witches burnt, the law
   enforced by torture,

the Cross of Christ a tower
   that is always falling —

sometimes burning,
   always falling.

Here I think of towers that fell
   a fortnight gone

and from those towers,
   shadows dropped

upon the broken matrices,
   as in a title reel by Bass.

Hitchcockian Girth

Like the omelette for breakfast yesterday
and the steak *tartare* the night before,

this *clafouti* is the best that I have
ever had. At home I will attempt

to diet although Novak assures me
that she prefers the fuller-figured male:

'In a man, the stomach is the seat of power.
I like them well-upholstered.'

Herrmann

Afternoon return — le Royal République

A hunted-looking advertising man
wearing an expensive well-cut suit

dashes in and darts a glance around.
Then his mobile chimes — the *North*

by Northwest overture. He palms it
to his ear, and takes the call outside.

Long after he has failed to reappear,
this man whose "O" stood for nothing,

a patron hums an urgent fragment,
wonders where she heard it.

Sometimes a Cigar

September 28th, 2001 — la Salle Pleyel

No call for an assassin in the gallery tonight.
To hear at last in this enormous room

Mahler's *Resurrection* live, has failed
to perturb my nothingness.

Afterwards I smoke like a client
who has mystified a courtesan.

I wish it were a Henry Clay
purloined from Doris Day's

own humidor, and sealed with
the menses of Eva Marie Saint. Instead

my pack of Gitanes, that unromantic
hypocrite, reminds me of the age.

Nuit gravement à la santé —
but if I die, I die.

Madeleine and Scottie

Gazing at *Amour and Psyche*
I feel an urge to expunge

myself, perhaps in the Seine –
a drowning welcome as rarely

before; and how am I supposed
to know what they feel about

La Joconde, that smirker,
stealing their thunder?

Would they like to murder her?
But no. They are in love

and even the Mona Lisa
cannot steal that; and even love

used to be something.
It used to be something.

Novak Mons

Tonight I will climb to the roof of the Louvre
and I will fall and Hitchcock will film it

his first science fiction and I am the
astronaut who has been nowhere

the rumour of an astronaut
dropped against the grid

his body a silhouette
falling endlessly

back into
the past

fin.

PATRICK CHAPMAN was born in 1968. *Slow Clocks of Decay* follows *Jazztown* (1991), *The New Pornography* (1996), *The Wow Signal* (2007), *Breaking Hearts and Traffic Lights* (2007), *A Shopping Mall on Mars* (2008), *The Darwin Vampires* (2010), *A Promiscuity of Spines: New & Selected Poems* (2012) and *The Negative Cutter* (2014). He has also written an award-winning short film starring Gina McKee and Aidan Gillen; and many episodes for children's animated television series broadcast around the world. His audio credits include writing adventures for *Doctor Who* and *Dan Dare*, and producing B7's 2014 dramatisation of Ray Bradbury's *The Martian Chronicles* for BBC Radio 4. This starred Derek Jacobi and Hayley Atwell, and won Silver at the 2015 New York Festivals World's Best Radio Programs. Chapman's writing has won first prize in the Cinescape Genre Literary Competition, been shortlisted twice in the Hennessy Awards, and received a nomination for a Pushcart Prize. 'Omertà' from this collection, was a runner-up in the 2016 WordsOnThe Waves Awards. With Dimitra Xidous he edits the poetry magazine *The Pickled Body*.